Mexican era

1823   Final period of construction begins on Tumacácori church
1828   April, last resident priest leaves Tumacácori
1836   Texas Independence
1840-43 Third Piman revolt
1843   Last resident Franciscan leaves San Ignacio
1845   Texas becomes part of the United States, Mexico declares war
1846-48 War; treaty of Guadalupe Hidalgo
1848   December, Tubac and Tumacácori abandoned

United States era

1854   Gadsden purchase adds southern Arizona to United States
1886   Geronimo surrenders for the last time
1908   September 15, Tumacacori National Monument established
1912   Arizona becomes a state
1916   National Park Service established
1919   Cleanup and stabilization begins at Tumacácori
1934-35 Archeological project at Tumacácori
1937   Visitor center built at Tumacácori
1975-82 Major stabilization project at Tumacácori

TUMACACORI

from Ranchería to National Monument

by

Nicholas J. Bleser

ISBN: 0-911408-84-3
LC: 89-061675
Editorial: T.J. Priehs
Design: Carole Thickstun
Illustration: Lawrence Ormsby
Production: Carole Thickstun, T.J. Priehs

PHOTOGRAPHY CREDITS

Pages 1, 5, 8, 14, 24-25, 26, 39: Carole Thickstun
Page 10: National Park Service
Page 15: George Roskruge
Pages 17, 21, 33: George Grant
Page 21: Walter Atwell
Page 36: Frank Pinkley
Page 37: Army photographer in 1899
Page 40: Unknown
Page 43: Nick Bleser
Page 44: Dave Forgang

ILLUSTRATION CREDITS

Cover, title page, pages 29, 35, 47: Lawrence Ormsby
Page 3: May Blas
Page 11: A. Severy
Page 12: Unknown, courtesy of Dept. of Colonial Monuments, Mexico
Page 20: J.H. Tovrea's plan, photographed by Louis R. Caywood
Pages 22, 23, 27, 30, 31: Cal Peters
Page 28: H.M.T. Powell
Pages 42, 43 From "Historic Structure Report: Tumacacori National Monu-
*   ment" by Anthony Crosby*

TUMACACORI *(too ma ká ko ri)*
IN OLD PIMA, TWO WORDS: A "ROCK" &

"flat," or "place of the flat rock." Also two words in modern Tohono

O'odham: an arch, a fold or bend, and the lighter colored material in that fold, descriptive of a geological formation on the east side of Tumacacori Peak near its base.

Tumacacori National Monument, nineteen miles north of the United States and Mexican Boundary, was established in 1908 to preserve and protect the physical remains of an eighteenth century Hispanic mission community. Visitors are impressed by the peace and tranquility of the silent ruins, but they remain somehow vaguely aware that such serenity may not always have been the case.

Come, then, on a brief journey into the past…

CHAPTER ONE
A New World for Spain

IN 1478, SPAIN CHAL-
LENGED PORTUGAL'S DOMINANCE OF
THE AFRICAN TRADE AND LOST. THUS ENCOURAGED TO

steer west in search of spices, and renewed by freedom from nearly eight centuries of Islamic occupation, Spain sailed into the unknown. One short generation later, the powerful Aztec nation lay in shattered ruins, defeated by the *conquistadores*.

Ever restless, and in the name of God, glory, and gold, these Spanish conquerors spread northwest in search of new lands and peoples. In 1528, a great Spanish expedition headed by Pánfilo de Narvaez landed on Florida's shores. Eight years later, the four sole survivors of that expedition, including Alvar Núñez Cabeza de Vaca and Esteban the Moor, walked into a Spanish town on the west coast of Mexico. Stories they told fed the imagination of the Viceroy of New Spain, who assigned a Franciscan friar named Marcos de Niza to go north in search of new lands and peoples. In 1539, with Esteban as his guide, Father Marcos and fellow expeditioners made their way into what today is Arizona to within sight of the Zuni Indian villages in New Mexico. Esteban was killed by the Zunis, but the Franciscan priest returned to Mexico with wondrous tales to tell.

In 1540, Marcos de Niza became the guide for a much larger expedition commanded by Francisco Vásquez de Coronado. They arrived at one of the Zuni pueblos in July 1540, where the Zunis rejected them. Coronado took the settlement by force. The European conquest of the Southwest had begun.

Coronado eventually perceived there were none of the advertised golden cities. Nor, as it turned out, was there much immediate glory. But fellow Spaniards working in support of his enterprise expanded Europeans' knowledge of the landscape. Hernando de Alarcón explored the Lower Colorado River with ships filled with supplies intended for Coronado. Melchior Díaz, looking for Alarcón, crossed the Colorado to become the first European to set foot on land that more than three centuries later was to become the State of California. Another of Coronado's men, García López de Cárdenas, reached the Grand Canyon, and Pedro de Tovar visited Hopi Indian country. Hernando de Alvarado went to Acoma, Taos, and Pecos pueblos and onto the plains of Texas. Through Oklahoma and into Kansas, searching for the elusive golden city of Quivira, went Coronado and his men. Theirs was a two-year odyssey that ended in 1542 with their return to Mexico. No doubt the Piman Indians at Tumacácori and neighboring Guevavi took note, and waited.

Spanish conquest was not a methodical progression northward at so many planned leagues a day. It was subject to every unforeseen contingency imaginable, including silver strikes, insurrections, and political whim. Some natives welcomed Spaniards, while others fought to the death. Still others accepted, then rebelled, and finally acquiesced. In northwestern New Spain, the Opata

2

and Lower Pima Indians of Sonora gradually accepted Christianity and the Spaniards. Because there were not enough priests to live among them, some thousand Lower Pimas had even moved southward to live in mission communities. The Yaqui Indians, too, accepted the teachings of the Jesuits, but for the next three centuries they would resist the governments of Spain and Mexico. The Tepehuan Indians of Chihuahua revolted in 1616 and severely slowed the Spanish advance as did the Pueblo Indians of New Mexico when they successfully rebelled in 1680. The Yaquis did likewise in 1740.

The natives of Tumacácori and other Northern Piman Indians never functioned as a unit, and rebellion, when it inevitably arrived, tended to be localized, fragmented, and of short duration.

Useful generalization is impossible. Some individuals accepted the blandishments of Spaniards and some refused. But Spain persevered.

CHAPTER TWO

The Spanish Mission System

SPAIN REMAINED A
BASTION OF CONSERVATIVE CATHOLICISM
DURING THE SIXTEENTH AND SEVENTEENTH-CENTURY STORM

of protest from those demanding church reform. Her militant Catholicism sprang from the holy crusades of the Middle Ages, a soldier's war against the infidel. The cross became a sword of fine Toledo steel. With the defeat of the Moors in Iberia and with the discovery of what was for her a New World, she looked west to millions of new souls. Here was a potential harvest guaranteed to fan the flames of missionary zeal.

Spain's efforts at domination were unique among Old World powers vying for influence in the New World. France and Russia exploited the natives for use in the fur trade, while England and her inheritors swept them aside or buried them, making room for more colonists. Spain alone, as a matter of national policy, attempted to incorporate the native Americans into her empire, to convert them to Christianity and thereby to change them into loyal taxpaying subjects of the Crown.

At the vanguard of these efforts were priests who were members of missionary orders, so-called regular clergy. As agents of the Crown whose salaries were paid from the Royal Treasury, the missionaries were expected to contact the natives and, in ten years' time from initial contact, to bring them to Christianity and vassalage. When the decade was up, the missionary was supposed to move on, turning the religious reins over to a secular priest who would be dependent for his support on his taxpaying parishioners. So long as natives were under the missionary's care, they remained exempt from taxes.

While all of this may have looked good on paper, the system failed in much of the eighteenth-century northern frontier of New Spain. Villages such as Tumacácori and neighboring Guevavi and Calabazas remained in mission status — and a drain on the Royal Treasury — either until

they were abandoned or to the end of the colonial period.

An important aspect of the Spanish mission system was its self-assured cultural insularity. Spaniards, and Europeans working for Spain, arrived among native Americans with systems of political organization based on centuries of conquest and feudal loyalty. Failing even to perceive a need to do so, Spaniards generally made little attempt to comprehend the Indians' ways of life. The basic Spanish assumption was that the Indians either had no political organization or that which they did have was a primitive and inferior version of the Spanish or other European systems. In the minds of Spaniards, what was being asked of the natives was quite simple: recognize the king as owner of all the land and as the supreme authority on earth; accept a simplified local system of Spanish government; accept Christianity (in the form of Catholicism); and recognize the missionaries as their spiritual and moral leaders.

It is difficult to know how Indians viewed these attempted impositions. They were being invited to accept the premise that some man, a mere mortal who lived in some far away place, now owned the land and may or may not permit them to use it as they saw fit. It was also possible, since this man was described as having great power, he might be a supernatural being — which would greatly complicate matters. The Indians were further being asked to work and fight for this invisible but powerful man, in return for which he would "protect" them. Until then they probably thought they had been doing quite well without such protection. Moreover, Spanish religious rules and precepts as well as legal codes and regulations were in conflict with traditional

*S*tatue of St. Francis of Assisi, founder of the Order of Friars Minor (Franciscans), carved in Mexico before 1785. Located in Tumacacori National Monument visitor center museum.

notions of moral leadership and government by consensus. They were being asked to adhere to a written code, generated through centuries of development in an alien culture, that one could neither talk to nor reason with.

The missionaries believed native Americans could be isolated in mission communities where they would be free of the distracting, and often immoral, influences of Spanish settlers and soldiers. Living in such communities, they would be taught by the priest and would live under his benign and civilizing influence. In some parts of the New World, as in Upper California, natives were forced by the Spanish military to move from their widely-scattered settlements and to concentrate their numbers in a comparatively few and crowded mission communities. This was the Spanish program of "reduction," reducing the amount of territory over which natives roamed and in which they lived. In such places as New Mexico, however, where there were already large and permanent settlements which the Spaniards called *pueblos*, and in the Pimería Alta where there were large *rancherías* along the rivers, there was no pressing need for reduction. Here, rather than being called "reductions," the mission communities were called "conversions." Mission churches were constructed where most people already lived.

Had the missions in northern New Spain moved beyond the stage of "reduction" or "conversion" in the plan for assimilation, which most did not, they would next have become *doctrinas* where the natives, who had become Christians, would receive instructions in the finer points of the doctrines of the Church. And, at last, they would heave been secularized, served by secular clergy in *curatos*, or curacies.

Just as missionaries were at the vanguard of efforts to assimilate the natives, so were they the vanguards of unintended tragedy. They, the soldiers who escorted them, and other Europeans were those who introduced Old World diseases against which the natives had developed no natural immunity. Smallpox, typhus and measles took a dreadful toll. Some scholars have estimated that the population of Mexico was 25,000,000 in 1520,

but that by 1605 it had plummeted to just over 1,000,000 — a staggering 86% loss. It took another 345 years, until 1950, before the population again reached 25,000,000. The sinister enemy of epidemic disease had an enormously disruptive effect on the societies and economies of the native peoples as it raced along with, and even ahead of, the invaders. To everyone's despair, established towns and frontier mission communities were periodically depopulated.

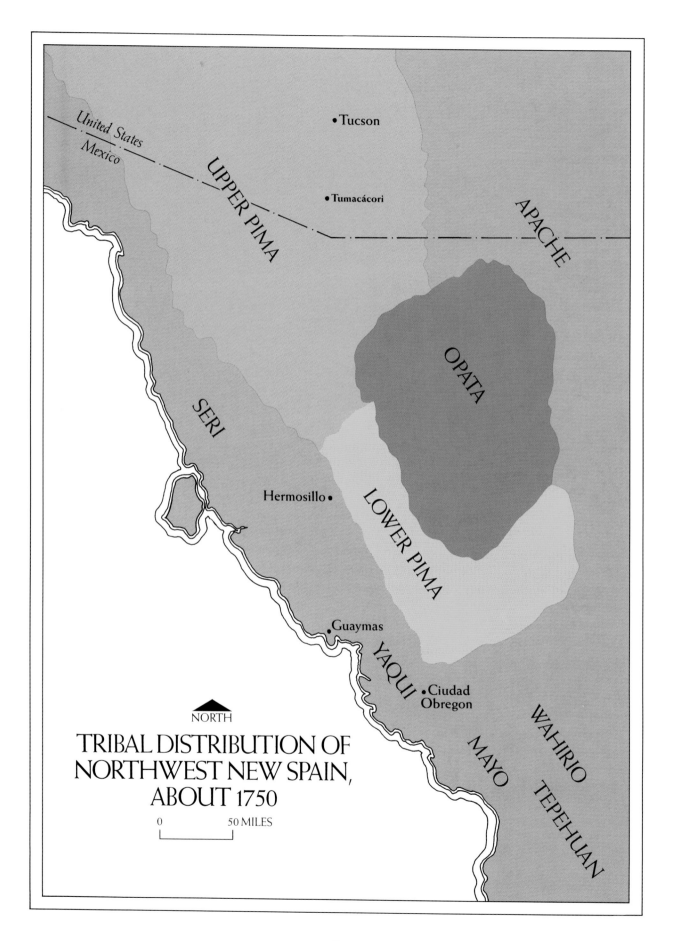

United States
Mexico

• Tucson

UPPER PIMA

• Tumacácori

APACHE

OPATA

SERI

LOWER PIMA

Hermosillo •

• Guaymas

YAQUI

• Ciudad
Obregon

WAHIRIO

MAYO

TEPEHUAN

NORTH

TRIBAL DISTRIBUTION OF
NORTHWEST NEW SPAIN,
ABOUT 1750

0   50 MILES

CHAPTER THREE
The Pimans (O'odham)

THE INDIANS WHOM
OUTSIDERS CALL "PIMAN," BUT WHO
UNIVERSALLY REFER TO THEMSELVES AS O'ODHAM, A TERM

which in their language means "people," formerly lived in an area stretching for a thousand miles from Arizona's Gila River on the north to northern Jalisco in the south. The southern groups were labeled by Spaniards as Tepecanos, Tepehuanes, and Nevomes or Pimas Bajos ("Lower Pimas" or "Southern Pimans"). Those in the north in what are today northern Sonora and southern Arizona were lumped together as the Pimas Altos ("Upper Pimas" or "Northern Pimans") and their lands came to be mapped as the "Pimería Alta." Among them were many sub-groups, all of whom spoke mutually intelligible dialects of the Piman language, whom the Spaniards referred to as Pimas, Sobas, Sobaipuris, Papagos, Gilenos, Kohatk, and Piatos. Their living descendants are people whom today we know as the Pimas and Tohono O'odham ("Desert People," or Papagos).

The origins of the Northern Pimans remain a mystery, but they may have worked their way northwest from the direction of Jalisco over the centuries, taking over lands abandoned by others such as the prehistoric Hohokam. Another of many possibilities is that they have been in the region since time immemorial, and that the Hohokam were invaders from the south whose society collapsed in the fifteenth century, leaving the Pimas in place.

When the Spaniards arrived in their lands in the seventeenth century, both the Lower and Upper Pimas seemed to be experiencing pressures from Opata Indians on the east and the Yaqui and Seri Indians who lived along the west coast of Sonora. Athapaskan-speaking Apache Indians would soon bring pressure to bear from the north and northeast, in time becoming the most tenacious foes of Spanish, Mexican, and Anglo efforts to settle this region. Little is known about these Apaches

before 1650, but they were destined to play a large role in Piman history.

Although the native peoples of the Pimería Alta shared a common language as well as additional common elements of culture, depending on where they lived in the Sonoran Desert and its adjacent lands they had distinctive economies and settlement patterns. In the far west, they were village-less nomadic gatherers and hunters. In the central portion of the Pimería Alta, where there are no permanent streams and where most of the Tohono O'odham Reservation is today, they were hunters, gatherers, and small-scale farmers who depended on summer rains and flash floods to grow modest crops of squashes, corn, and tepary beans. These people typically moved seasonally between two rancherías, one located by fields in an intermontane valley where summer crops were grown and a second located near a permanent spring in the foothills where water could be obtained during winter. The ranchería was a collection of dome-shaped brush houses located as much as a half mile from each other but always within hearing distance of the village crier who climbed to the top of the "rain house" or "big house," the community's only communal structure, to shout instructions for the day's activities.

On the northern, eastern, and southern perimeters of the Pimería Alta were permanent streams. Here, where a year around supply of water was assured, the desert life of plants, man, and other animals assumed its most luxuriant form. People could, and did, live more-or-less permanently in single rancherías situated next to rivers. The numbers of Pimans here were the greatest, their rancherías the largest. In the summer they could rely on the rivers' floodplains for their agricultural fields, and if they had summer field settlements in addition to permanent winter homes, such field villages were never very far away.

It is no accident that all Pimería Alta missions which came to have resident priests were located in these riverine rancherías. Here were the most souls to be saved; here were an assured supply of food and water; and, since rivers in the deserts are highways, here were stopping points on the main routes of commerce and supply.

Peacetime political organization among the Northern Pimans was at the village level or, at most, among a group of related villages which had splintered off from a parent village. A village leader was expected to be a wise and knowledgeable man, a person who could speak well in council and who could mediate disputes and command respect. Governance was by consensus of adult males. The leader had no autocratic powers; his were the powers of persuasion. The strength of a community lay in mutual cooperation and in the ability of its members to recognize the wisdom leading to a unanimous decision.

Organization in times of war was a different matter. Peacetime government was virtually ignored, and autocratic authority was invested in the war leader, a man known for his bravery, fighting abilities, and effective magic. War leaders became temporary commanders able to make swift and effective decisions in the crises of defense or attack. Some such leaders assumed power beyond the limits of their villages or related villages and were acknowledged by their fellow O'odham throughout much of the Pimería Alta.

Santa Cruz River after summer storm

8

CHAPTER FOUR

Kino & the Northern Pimans

EUSEBIO FRANCISCO
KINO, THE NAME IS SYNONYMOUS WITH
NORTHERN SONORA AND SOUTHERN ARIZONA. KINO WAS A

mathematician, cartographer, astronomer, explorer, priest, cattleman, and Jesuit missionary, an indefatigable dynamo of the late seventeenth and early eighteenth centuries. His name is used on enterprises unimagined three centuries ago, and the Tucson business directory is awash in Kinos even as are the business directories of Sonoran communities. His likeness appears on a Mexican postage stamp. The crypt covering his mortal remains has become a shrine in the Sonora city to which his name has been added, Magdalena de Kino. Statues of him appear in places he never visited as well as in many he did. The earliest of these were done in 1936. One, a handsome bas-relief commissioned by the Kino Memorial Association, stands at the northwest corner of City Hall in Tucson. It shows an Indian, presumably Piman, leading Kino north on foot. The other, a 28″ high bronze equestrian statue sculptured by Eugene Morahan, was commissioned by the National Park Service for Tumacacori National Monument. Today there are dozens of likenesses of Kino, both statues and paintings, on public display in communities from Hermosillo, the capital of Sonora, to Phoenix, the capital of Arizona, as well as in Statuary Hall in the United States Capitol in Washington, D.C.

Kino was born, raised, and educated in the Holy Roman Empire. Home was the northern Italian Tyrol in the Val di Non, near Segno. The family name has gone through phonetic changes from Chino (pronounced Kino in Italian) to modern Chini, but Eusebio opted for a pronounceable Spanish spelling when he became a missionary for Spain. Educated in Trent as well as in Germany, neither far from home, he promised to dedicate his life to St. Francis Xavier and to the Jesuits if cured from a severe illness, adding Francisco to his name upon

recovery. He hoped to go to the Orient but drew New Spain, and in 1681 he arrived in Mexico.

How is it that an Italian-born, German-educated Jesuit came to work for the King of Spain?

Spaniards had a deep distrust of strangers, as did the French and Germans. Too often the foreigner had arrived in their lands as an invader. Spanish pride in the early sixteenth century took an anti-foreign turn. The Moors had been defeated, recalcitrant Jews driven into exile, a new world discovered, and the country united under a strong leadership. The official policy of Spain was to exclude foreigners from the New World unless they met stringent requirements. There were three principal reasons: political security of the colonial empire, the monopoly of trade with the colonies, and the preservation of orthodox Catholicism. Enforcement of any official policy, however, is seldom uniform. So it was in the vast expanse of the New World, and the rules were relaxed in the case of those with needed skills if they came from friendly or weaker nations.

Secure in their roles as guardians of Catholicism, the religious orders tended to be cosmopolitan in their composition, especially the Society of Jesus (i.e., the Jesuits). Thus it is that we find missionaries in the historical records of northwestern New Spain with such names as Pfefferkorn, Sedelmayr, Nentvig, Segesser, Pauer, Rapicani, Grazhofer, and Kino. There were, of course, Spaniards as well.

By March of 1687 when Kino arrived as the first missionary assigned permanently to work in the Pimería Alta, he had been tested and frustrated in attempts to establish missions in Baja California. The blunders of soldiers and civilians as well as the lack of food and water had doomed these early efforts, but the missionary hoped to return. The Seri Indians on the Sonoran coast had asked him to stay during a visit there, and since California had been temporarily abandoned, he sought and received both permission and financial backing to carry out work on the mainland. Here, he believed, it would be possible to raise livestock and crops with which California missions could be supplied. There was an added proviso, however: the Pimas of the north

*S*eri Indians at Desemboque, Sonora in 1946 living a lifestyle similar to the Pimas at Tumacácori

would have to be included in the plans. Kino was ordered by the Jesuit Father Provincial "to undertake the conversion of the heathen Pima Indians in this North America."

He went to Oposura (now Moctezuma), Sonora, to confer with Father Visitor González. They traveled together to Cucurpe, an Opata Indian mission settlement where Father José de Aguilar was in residence. Cucurpe was a few miles downstream on the Río San Miguel from where Kino was about to plant the seed of Christianity and of Spain among the Northern Pimans.

On March 13, 1687, Kino and fathers Aguilar and González rode north from Cucurpe to the Piman village of Cosari, or Bamotze, as it was sometimes called. It was here that Kino made his headquarters, renaming the place Nuestra Señora de los Dolores, Our Lady of Sorrows. From Dolores he would travel to all corners of the Pimería during the twenty-four years left to him.

Kino's writings exude enthusiasm. He never tired of expounding the virtues of the people in the Pimería, but he seldom told much about them as individuals. Neither did he describe the characteristics of Piman culture in an objective way. Much of his writing seems intended to sell outsiders on the value of his enterprise.

It is clear, however, that he was a patient man. He did not judge the cultural traits of others by his own as did, and do, so many. Derogatory adjectives were not part of his vocabulary in describing Pimans, although, like other missionaries of his era, he consistently conceptualized them as adult children. Missionaries were, after all, "fathers," and the uninitiated were children of their flock who, because they were "children," could not be held fully accountable for all their actions.

Kino would sit for hours or days, ignoring schedules, patiently discussing, teaching, or listening until the demands of various leaders were met and all were satisfied. His methods of discussion and persuasion, and his desire to arrive at consensus, were like those of the moral leaders of the Pimans. This fact, combined with his organizational skills and ability to utilize the talents of others, placed him in high esteem among his Piman friends.

CHAPTER FIVE

Tumacácori Greets the Missionaries

THERE HAD BEEN SO MANY RUMORS, GOOD AND BAD, ABOUT HOW MATTERS WERE PROCEEDING IN PIMERÍA ALTA THAT THE

new Father Visitor, Juan María Salvatierra, decided to see for himself. He arrived at Nuestra Señora de los Dolores on Christmas Eve of 1690, and during the next months he and Kino visited the other three priests by then assigned to the Pimería. In January 1691, they were in Tucubavia, a Piman settlement about thirty miles southwest of Tumacácori. They were about to return in the direction of Dolores when Piman Indians couriers from the villages of San Xavier del Bac and Tumacácori "came to meet us," wrote Kino, "with some crosses which they gave us, kneeling with great veneration, and asking us on behalf of all their people to go to their rancherías also. The Father Visitor said to me that those crosses which they carried were tongues that spoke volumes and with great force, and that we could not fail to go where by means of them they called us."

Kino continued: "Whereupon we ascended to the Valley of Guevavi, a journey of about fifteen leagues, and arrived at the ranchería of San Cayetano del Tumacácori. In San Cayetano they had prepared us three arbors, one in which to say mass, another in which to sleep, and the third for a kitchen. There were more than forty houses close together. Some infants were baptized, and the Father Visitor gave good hopes to all that they should obtain the fathers, the holy baptism, and the boon of their eternal salvation which they requested. When his reverence had seen so many people, so docile and affable, with such beautiful, fertile, and pleasant valleys, inhabited by industrious Indians, he said to me these words: 'My Father Rector, not only shall the removal

from this Pimería of any of the four fathers assigned to it not be considered but four more shall come, and by divine grace I shall try to be one of them'.

"We went to the ranchería of Guevavi and to the valley and ranchería of Santa María [Soamca], a journey of fifteen leagues, where we remained five days, catechizing and baptizing infants and adults."

Father Visitor Salvatierra's enthusiasm for what he had seen is understandable. He and Kino believed the fertile Pimería would help support missionary efforts in Baja California. Kino would continue his work in the area, exploring new land routes for supply, and others would strengthen missionary efforts among the Pimans.

Why, however, did the Pimans seem so eager to have the Jesuits live among them? The Pimans have left us no written record of their motives, so one can only speculate. Surely new agricultural products were intriguing. These included cattle, sheep, horses, chickens, goats, fruit trees, and an interesting crop called wheat. Unlike corn, wheat could be grown in the winter.

The alien concept of monotheism and its attendant Catholic ritual observances may have been viewed as a good method for avoiding, as well as healing, afflictions. Its acceptance—on the surface, at least—may have seemed a small price to pay in return for metal tools and a more secure subsistence resulting from the addition of livestock and new crops.

Whatever the reasons, the Northern Pimans had welcomed Kino, and Spain, into their home.

CHAPTER SIX

Rebellion and a Massacre

ALTHOUGH THE
FATHER VISITOR HAD ASSURED
THE PEOPLE OF TUMACACORI AND GUEVAVI THEY WOULD SOON

have a priest of their own, "soon" was a relative word. Available missionaries remained in short supply and other matters, some of them tragic, intervened.

Through the first half of the 1690s, Pimans in mission settlements south of Tumacácori and Guevavi accepted conversion in growing numbers. On one occasion they even allied themselves with Spanish soldiers and Opata Indians to fend off an attack from the northeast by hostile Jocomes and Apaches. As mission cattle herds and cultivated fields became abundant, they proved to be an irresistible target for nomadic hunters like Apaches.

In 1695, Kino was forced to draw on all his reserves of good will, patience, tolerance, and persuasion. The problems began at the mission of Tubutama in the Altar Valley where Father Daniel Januske was stationed. Father Januske was following standard procedure when he asked for Spanish soldiers to come to his settlement to punish two Pimans who were haranguing their fellows and who were, he believed, threatening his life. The military complied, and the Indians were punished "in sight of the rest," possibly hanged. So was Father Januske following procedure when he employed a Christianized Indian as overseer of the mission's herds and fields. He was an Opata, an apparently arrogant individual who looked on the Pimans as being something worse than country dolts, people whom he could kick and otherwise abuse. In March of 1695, when Father Januske was away, the Tubutama natives released their pent up anger by murdering the overseer as well as two other Opatas who happened to be there at the time. They burned the priest's house and the church, desecrated sacred artifacts,

and killed cattle belonging to the mission. A band of these rebels headed south, enlisting more Pimas to their cause at the villages of Oquitoa and Pitiquito. In early April they reached the mission settlement at Caborca where they killed the resident missionary, Father Francisco Saeta. Father Saeta became the Jesuits' first martyr in the Pimería Alta.

The soldiers responded quickly to the crisis, but could find no organized enemy to fight. Because it appeared there was no general uprising, they opted for negotiation. Father Kino was asked to assemble those leaders who had not taken part in the rebellion and to ask them to name the guilty parties. A meeting among Pimans, Kino, Spanish soldiers, and Seri Indian allies took place at the ranchería of El Tupo. All went well until the first guilty man was pointed out. Instead of being arrested, he was summarily beheaded by one of the officers. Panic! Most of the fifty Pimans killed in the ensuing melee were peaceful ones. Now the Spaniards had a real war on their hands.

The remaining mission buildings at Tubutama and Caborca were burned. Next the same happened to the chapels and other structures at Imuris, Magdalena, and San Ignacio. Again the soldiers arrived, reinforced this time by Piman allies, and again they could find no one to fight. Piman leaders were anxious for peace, and once more Kino arranged a meeting at El Tupo, now called *La Matanza* (The Slaughter) by most. This time cooler heads prevailed and peace returned. The incident would be remembered two generations later, however, during a second and more devastating Piman rebellion.

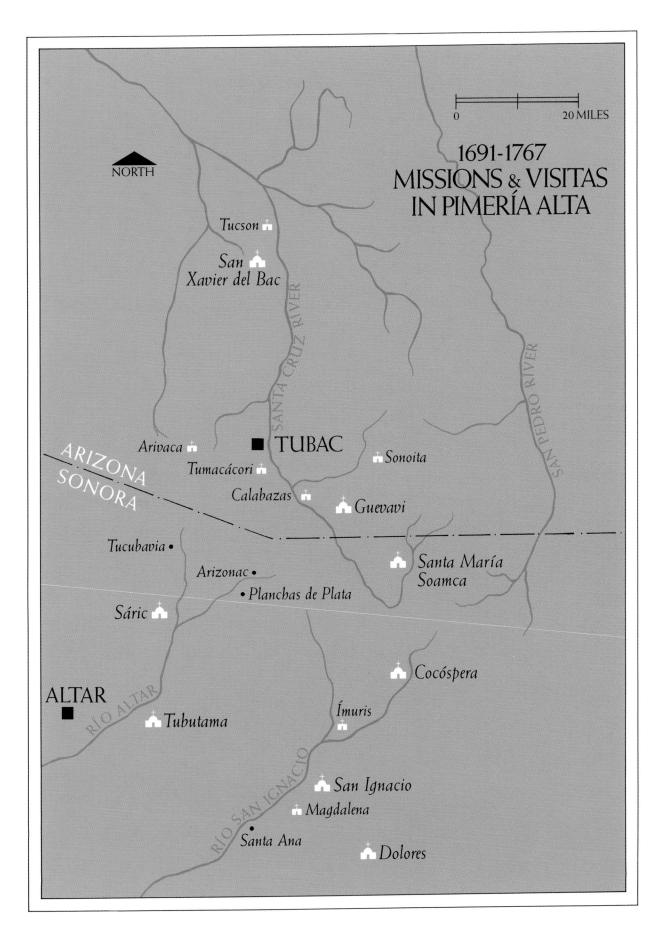

0   20 MILES

1691-1767
MISSIONS & VISITAS
IN PIMERÍA ALTA

NORTH

Tucson

San
Xavier del Bac

SANTA CRUZ RIVER

SAN PEDRO RIVER

Arivaca

■ TUBAC

Sonoita

ARIZONA
SONORA

Tumacácori

Calabazas

Guevavi

Tucubavia •

Arizonac •

Santa María
Soamca

• Planchas de Plata

Sáric

Cocóspera

ALTAR

RÍO ALTAR

Tubutama

Ímuris

RÍO SAN IGNACIO

San Ignacio

Magdalena

•
Santa Ana

Dolores

CHAPTER SEVEN

Tumacácori's Mission Beginnings

THERE WERE NOT
ENOUGH PRIESTS TO WORK IN ALL THE
VILLAGES & MOST WOULD NEVER SEE A RESIDENT JESUIT. ATTEMPTS

in 1701 to establish a district headquarters (*cabecera*) at Guevavi, fifteen miles upstream from Tumacácori, could hardly be called successful. The first resident missionary, Juan de San Martín, lasted less than a year. He stayed only long enough to build "a small but neat house and church" before illness forced him to move. It would be another thirty years before the Jesuits would settle in.

It fell to Kino once again, operating from his mission at Dolores, to serve the people at the non-functional cabecera and its three visiting stations, or *visitas*, within a twenty-five mile radius: San Cayetano de Tumacácori to the north, San Luis Bacoancos to the south, and los Santos Reyes de Sonoita to the east. San Xavier del Bac

was added as a visita in August 1702, when its first resident priest became sick and died. Nine years later, Kino, too, was dead. While dedicating a new chapel to San Francisco Xavier in Magdalena be became ill and died about midnight on March 15, 1711. He was sixty-five.

Other Jesuits arrived at some of the mission stations in the Altar Valley, and Luis Xavier Velarde was at Cocospera, north of Dolores. But for the two decades following Kino's death, missions in the Santa Cruz Valley became the responsibility of sturdy Agustín de Campos, the missionary at San Ignacio. In just four years, from 1716 to 1720, he recorded 1,004 baptisms, mostly children. During one trip north in April, 1726, he paused

to rest and baptized a baby brought to him from the adjacent village, recording for the first time the name of Tumacácori's northern neighbor, the ranchería of Tubac. A persistent and seemingly tireless man of God, Campos kept the flame of Christianity alive in the northern Pimería and would serve more than forty years at San Ignacio before dying of the infirmities of old age enroute to Chihuahua in 1737.

Wars in Europe had their eventual effect on the frontier. With the new Bourbon King of Spain, Philip V, a surge of vitality roused the Spanish Empire. More regular clergy were sent to the north and the cabecera of Guevavi finally got its series of resident missionaries beginning in 1732. From then until 1767, when the Jesuits were expelled from New Spain by the Crown, Guevavi and its visitas would be increasingly better attended. A unique discovery of silver in October, 1736 at the nearby mining camp of Arizonac was spectacular but short-lived. The *planchas de plata* (slabs of silver) that had been found there on the ground's surface vanished quickly. Left behind were dreams of getting rich quickly, an enhanced Spanish interest in the far north, and the name of a future state.

The Arizonac find had its effect on Guevavi. More people, including Spaniards, arrived in its environs.

Unless one stops to listen to the ghosts within them, Guevavi's adobe walls might seem to be just part of a silent ruin. These gray-colored mud bricks, however, heard the sounds of festival and feast, the moans of agony and death, and childrens' laughter. They witnessed life, smelled it, and tasted it: mesquite smoke and church incense, fresh hot corn tortillas, summer rains. And they were listening, too, that November day in 1751, when bloodied Tubac foreman Juan de Figueroa brought reports of Pimans in revolt.

Roused and led by the obviously angry Luis Oacpicagigua, a native of Sáric in the Altar Valley, Pimans, chafing at the Spanish bit, laid waste to Arivaca, a newly-added visita of Guevavi to the west. They killed two priests and more than a hundred settlers, miners, and herdsmen. They destroyed buildings at Guevavi, San Xavier, and Tubac. As Spaniards fled south, more Pimans joined Luis while others waited in the mountains for the struggle to end. Four months after the debacle began, Luis surrendered to the Spanish soldiers. But for years afterwards a few disenchanted Pimans would now and then join forces with anti-Spanish Seris and Apaches, raiding ranches and missions, disrupting lives and instilling fear.

*T*he ruins of district headquarters or cabecera of Guevavi as they appeared when photographed in 1889

In the wake of the 1751 rebellion, it was decided that a *presidio*, a military outpost, should be built at Tubac. The native inhabitants of this small village would be joined with those of Tumacácori in a settlement which would also be known as Tumacácori, but with a different patron saint. A new location on the west side of the river was chosen, and about March 19 of 1753 the new mission visita of San José de Tumacácori was dedicated with suitable pomp and ceremony. The old village of San Cayetano de Tumacácori which Kino had known, situated on a crescent-shaped bend of the river on its east side in a grove of trees, was abandoned. Now both village and presidio would be on the same side of the river, three miles apart.

CHAPTER EIGHT

Tumacácori's Final Years as a Visita

BY 1757, FATHER FRAN-
CISCO XAVIER PAUER, WHO HAD ARRIVED
AT THE CABECERA OF GUEVAVI FOUR YEARS EARLIER, HAD BUILT

a new adobe church at Tumacácori. Roughly half the size of the present structure, this adobe building with its flat, *viga* (wood beam) roof served residents of the area for over sixty years. Measuring about sixty by twenty feet and with the entrance and *campo santo* (cemetery) at the east end, the sacristy and other rooms adjoined it on the south side. Its overall appearance resembled that of the Jesuit-built mission, still standing, at Oquitoa in the Altar Valley.

Church construction aside, mission populations, thanks largely to epidemic diseases, were on the decline. More and more the missions began to resemble reductions (*reducciones*) rather than conversions (*conversiones*), with Pimans who lived in the riverless desert to the west of the Santa Cruz Valley being encouraged to settle in mission communities to supplement the depleted numbers of their linguistic brethren. Then, in the 1760s, the Spaniards made a mistake. Northern Pimans whom the Spaniards called "Sobaipuris" were moved from their villages on the San Pedro River to the east. Settled anew in villages on the Santa Cruz and elsewhere, these Sobaipuris had provided a buffer against Apaches. Once they were resettled, the gate was opened wide to Apache incursions, and over the next twenty-five years raiding and warfare steadily increased.

Even today, a century after conflict with Pimans, Spaniards, Mexicans, and Anglos, the name "Apache" still evokes emotions. Primarily hunters and gatherers, over centuries these skilled survivors came to know every route, pass, canyon, and water hole along their route of gradual migration south from Alaska and Canada. They lived in extended family groups centering around the residence of the wife's family. Local groups comprised of a number of extended families had male leaders who achieved their status through such personal traits as bravery, generosity, and eloquence. So long as he retained his powers of persuasion and his policies were successful, a leader continued in his role. As among Pimans, the job was not hereditary.

Although a subject of little interest to their victims, Apaches made a sharp distinction between raiding and warfare. The purpose of a raid, almost always carried out by a very few men, was to steal enemy horses and other supplies without encountering the enemy. If they were discovered and attacked, however, they would defend themselves, still hoping to escape with their booty and as few casualties as possible.

Warfare, on the other hand, was a deliberate act of revenge for previous casualties incurred. War parties tended to be large. The bravest act possible was to kill or capture an enemy. If the enemy were destroyed or routed, his camp would be looted, but this was not the principal goal of warfare.

Apaches had no enthusiasm for pursuing lost causes. If the battle were going badly, everyone scattered to regroup later at a prearranged location. Fear of spiritual contamination from a dead enemy was sufficiently powerful that there was no interest in scalping except to avenge a similar insult. Even then, only special warriors were allowed to take scalps.

Apaches were incredible guerrilla warriors. Whole families traveled fast and light, women and children tending camp while warriors attacked enemies and disappeared only to reappear in another strike a hundred miles away.

As if Apache raiding and warfare weren't enough

The facade of Oquitoa, a Jesuit-built mission in Sonora, having a similar appearance to the 1757 adobe church built at Tumacácori

turmoil for the frontier, the Society of Jesus was in trouble. Implicated in a plot to kill the King of Portugal, its members were banished from that empire. Next, the French expelled the Jesuits. Their enemies in Spain waited and finally made their case with Carlos III. The royal edict was sent to the far corners of the Spanish Empire: the Jesuits were to be expelled. A special courier brought the sealed orders to the Governor of Sonora, then from him to appointed presidial captains.

On July 23, 1767, the seals were broken and the roundup of priests began. Swiftly and with great care soldiers ordered each priest to gather his personal belongings, prepared inventories of mission properties, and locked all buildings. The Jesuits were launched on a long ordeal, a journey of more than a year to the port of Vera Cruz as prisoners. Some who survived were scattered throughout Spain in a state of arrest; others, non-Spaniards, returned to their countries of birth.

Suddenly, the priests were gone from the Pimería Alta. Left behind were communities whose people were ill prepared to govern themselves. Tubac's presidial commander, Captain Juan Bautista de Anza, wrote that after only six weeks of the Jesuits' departure most of the grain and livestock had disappeared from Tumacácori without being accounted for, and he had taken back the keys from the man left in charge. Finally, replacements for the Jesuits began to arrive in the summer of 1768. They were gray-robed Franciscans from the Apostolic College of Santa Cruz de Querétaro.

Friar Juan Crisóstomo Gil de Bernabé took over the declining cabecera at Guevavi. Returning from an illness, in September, he moved his headquarters to Tumacácori. Guevavi ended its long and troubled career as a mission, and Tumacácori would be a visita no more.

17

CHAPTER NINE

Franciscans at Tumacácori: The Eighteenth Century

THE SUPPLY OF PRIESTS FOR THE PIMERÍA ALTA INCREASED UNDER THE FRANCISCANS. EACH CABECERA ALWAYS HAD AT LEAST ONE

priest in residence; sometimes, two. Those who were the first to arrive generally failed to stay more than a few years. As the Indian population declined, missions were consolidated. Tumacácori had only Calabazas and Sonoita as visitas, and Sonoita gave up the ghost in 1773. Franciscan emphasis was placed on the Santa Cruz Valley settlements of Calabazas, Tumacácori, San Xavier, and the presidio at Tubac. Elsewhere, they stationed friars at San Ignacio, Magdalena, Cocóspera, Caborca, and communities on the Río Altar.

The Río Santa Cruz lay on the path of the empire. In 1775 Tumacácori and its resident priests, Tomás Eixarch and Pedro Antonio de Arriquibar, were witness to the passing of more than 240 soldiers, their family members, and other settlers enroute to Alta California in an expedition led by Juan Bautista de Anza. Some of these people were destined to become the founders of the city of San Francisco.

In April 1780, Baltazar Carrillo arrived as Tumacácori's priest. Until his death fifteen-and-a-half years later he would labor alone.

In May 1780, Royal engineer Geronimo de la Rocha wrote of his visit: "This village of Tumacácori is almost enclosed by walls on all four sides, to which are being added several small houses for more security. The village has very good fields, but they complain of having to cope with a scarcity of water during the dry period, and thus they hold back what there is and it does not get to Tubac."

Tubac had similar complaints. "We continued our march one league north to the old presidio of Tubac," wrote Rocha. "With reference to Tubac it has been reduced to nine residents who have presented themselves

to the Brigadier, telling him that they cannot continue to exist due to the total lack of water for cultivation, in addition to which the enemy committed hostilities against them. There are a sufficient number of houses, but these same houses are used as entrenchments by the Apaches from which to launch their attacks."

Smallpox killed ten percent of Tumacácori's residents in five short weeks during 1781. Father Carrillo buried as many victims of the epidemic, twenty-two, as would die of other causes during the next six years.

About the time Calabazas was abandoned as the last visita of Tumacácori, the Tubac presidio was reoccupied by Pima soldiers in the employ of Spain. Further, a new policy to deal with Apaches was implemented in 1786, one of peace. It was peace at a price, and it nearly succeeded.

When the realization finally came that these nomadic peoples were poor candidates for mission living (although a few did become assimilated into non-Indian culture), and when it became apparent they were all but impossible to defeat militarily, the Spaniards tried bribery. It had been observed that Apaches would make temporary peace to trade for guns, food, and horses and, moreover, that they could temporarily be enlisted as allies against other Apaches. Thus it became official Spanish policy to offer firearms, food, clothing, and liquor in an attempt to make Apaches dependent on presidios as their sources of supply. Dissension among various Apache groups was exploited as well. Those who refused to make peace were relentlessly pursued. The result was a decrease in raiding. It never stopped completely, but for more than forty years the frontier was a safer place than it had been.

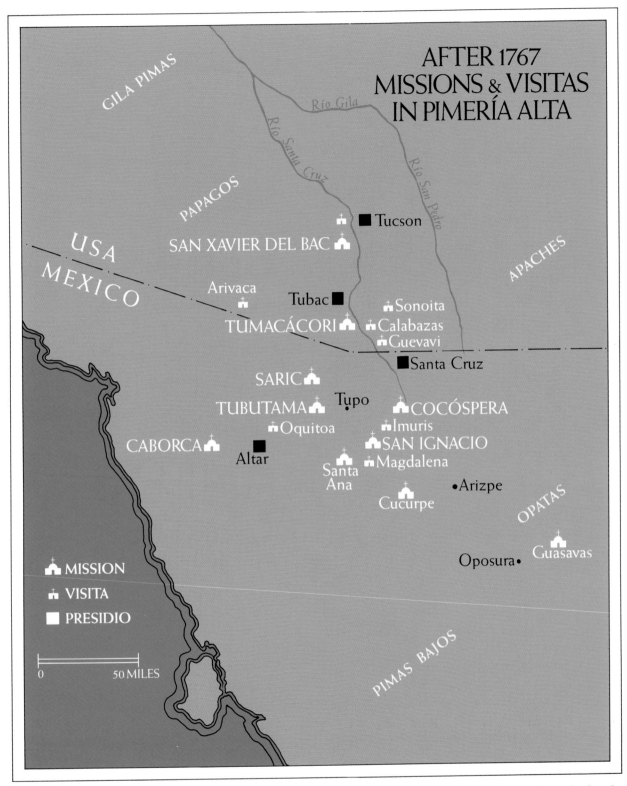

AFTER 1767
MISSIONS & VISITAS
IN PIMERÍA ALTA

GILA PIMAS

Río Gila

Río Santa Cruz

Río San Pedro

PAPAGOS

USA

MEXICO

APACHES

■ Tucson

SAN XAVIER DEL BAC

Arivaca

Tubac ■

Sonoita

TUMACÁCORI

Calabazas

Guevavi

■ Santa Cruz

SARIC

TUBUTAMA   Tupo   COCÓSPERA

Oquitoa   Imuris

CABORCA   SAN IGNACIO

Altar   Magdalena

Santa
Ana   •Arizpe

Cucurpe

OPATAS

Oposura•   Guasavas

MISSION

VISITA

PRESIDIO

0   50 MILES

PIMAS BAJOS

It was when the so-called "peace policy" was in effect, on Sunday, October 11, 1795, that Spanish-born Father Narcisco Gutiérrez buried Father Carrillo, his predecessor. The body was lowered into a grave in front of the altar in the small church of San José de Tumacácori. For the next quarter century one priest would again be in charge, but this time he would not be alone. A total of eight priests would assist him over the years. Of Tumacácori's century-and-a-half career as a mission community, the combined carers of fathers Carrillo and Gutiérrez would cover more than a fourth of it.

CHAPTER TEN

Work on a New Church Begins

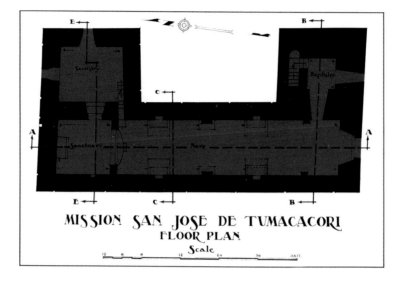

MISSION SAN JOSE DE TUMACACORI
FLOOR PLAN
Scale

THE MIGHT AND MAJESTY OF SPAIN'S ONCE POWERFUL EMPIRE

WAS WITHERING AS THE EIGHTEENTH CENTURY DREW TO A

close, but the dream of missionary expansion lived on at Tumacácori. It was frustrated, however, by the wars in Europe, by revolutions and new forms of government, and by realities at home. Not only did three men die, for example, but 1,360 sheep were wantonly slaughtered during an Apache attack on June 5, 1801. Whether this was raiding or warfare was probably not being strongly debated at the mission that day. The Apaches waited in vain, hoping to draw the people out into the open. It was not until the next afternoon that help arrived from Tubac. The three bodies could at least be given a decent burial.

A report on the state of the missions of the Pimería Alta was compiled in 1803, the same year that the United States nearly doubled in size via the Louisiana Purchase, an area once claimed by Spain. Half a dozen new churches had been built by the Franciscans, and

only Caborca and Tumacácori were pronounced substandard. Construction was about to start at the former, and at Tumacácori a church was "currently being built anew." Both were to be patterned after the magnificent Franciscan-built structure at Mission San Xavier del Bac. Caborca would win the race to completion.

Father Gutiérrez had somehow found money for work at Tumacácori. In 1801 he had hired a *maestro de albañil*, or master mason, to come up with a set of plans. The church, with five-foot thick foundations, would be in the shape of a cross, with a main entrance at the south end, a dome over the crossing and barrel vaults over the nave, transepts, and sacristy. A southeast bell tower, one with foundations nine feet thick instead of five and with an interior stairway, would buttress the vaulted choir loft. To balance the facade and to buttress the southwest corner, another tower was needed. For whatever reasons, it was eliminated from the plan and never built.

The principal building material would be adobes. *Adobe* is a Spanish word with roots in Arabic. It has come to mean three things: sun-dried mud bricks; the earth that forms the mud; and a structure made of such bricks. It is possibly the world's oldest manufactured building material. References to "brick" in ancient documents, including the Bible, are to mud bricks. The smelters of King Solomon's mines contained adobes. It is a simple material, easy to make, and forgiving to work with.

Construction began in 1802. The maestro hired an assistant and the necessary skilled laborers to burn lime and make adobes, a total crew of from eighteen to twenty, with unskilled labor coming from the village as needed. Measuring west from the southwest corner of the convento, the maestro pegged out the foundation trenches. They were dug to a depth of three feet. River boulders both great and small were hauled to the site, some to be used for facing and others for the carefully-laid rubble core. Fortunately, the soil at Tumacácori is good just above the floodplain, not as rocky as that even a hundred yards farther west. It is suitable for adobes and for mud mortar. The soil for the adobes probably came from an area just east of the convento where the mission garden and orchard were located. The irrigation ditch would have furnished the necessary water and the location is close to the construction site.

By the end of 1802, the cobblestone foundation was above ground, but the money was spent. To protect them from weathering, the two-foot high foundations had two courses of adobes laid on top of them and the surfaces were plastered inside and out with decorative handfuls of crushed burned brick pressed into the wet plaster.

The model for all this, Mission San Xavier del Bac, had cost more than $30,000 pesos, which in 1797, when the church was finished, equalled 6,000 head of cattle. By 1803 the price had fallen, and a cow was worth only $3-1/2 pesos. But the maestro and his crew alone cost $9 pesos a day, to which had to be added the cost of tools and materials. Tumacácori's population had increased 70% between 1801 and 1802, some of it due to construction and some because of an increase in mining and other activities in the region. The 1802 rolls indicate 76 Indians and 102 "Spaniards," some of the latter no doubt racially mixed.

As Father Gutiérrez fretted about funding, and managed to add a few adobes to his church even without funding,

*A*dobe making in 1934, as it was done during construction in 1802

the vaults on the new church at Caborca were being built in 1805. Caborca's census for that year showed an increase of thirty "Spaniards," while Tumacácori lost twenty. The maestro and his crew had followed the jobs. A frustrated Gutiérrez had to continue to make do with the tired old Jesuit church and a few courses of adobes on the new one as La Purísima Concepción de Nuestra Señora de Caborca was dedicated in May 1809. Where there had been two substandard churches, only one remained.

*S*an Xavier Mission near Tucson, as photographed in 1935 by George Grant

21

CHAPTER ELEVEN

The Daily Round

LIFE WENT ON AND
LIFE IN A FRANCISCAN MISSION COMMU-
NITY WAS REGULATED BY THE CLOCK IN THE PRIEST'S QUARTERS

and by bells. There were a minimum of two bells, a large one to signal spiritual matters and a small one to be rung in connection with the mundane duties of daily life. Tumacácori boasted four bells in its later years.

The day began at sunrise with the sound of a bell summoning everyone to the church for mass and prayers. About an hour later, the breakfast bell was rung. Then came the work bell. Everyone had assigned tasks, from working with the herds to gathering wood, cultivating the fields, or helping in the various shops. In the morning and again in the afternoon the children over five years of age were given religious instruction. The priests had their midday meal about 11:15 or 11:30.

From noon until two o'clock everyone had their meal and siesta. Then it was back to work until 5:00 p.m., when it was time again for prayers. After the evening meal there was a little free time before the final bell was rung at 8:00 p.m., signalling the end of another day.

Paternalistic though the system was, Narcisco Gutiérrez did not run it without help. Juan Legarra, a Piman Indian born at Guevavi in 1768, had been appointed Tumacácori's governor in 1799. A rigid system of organization and government was one of many Spanish contributions to the new way of life. Assisting the priest and village governor were Spanish-appointed Indian officials with a variety of administrative and legal roles. So were there interpreters, a sacristán, cooks, houseboys, tortilla makers, overseers of the ox and goat herders, shepherds, an orchard keeper, and others — all of whom required close supervision and coordination. Life in the missions was not a simple matter of peace, quiet meditation, and silent prayer.

CHAPTER TWELVE
A Land Grant

Toward the end of 1806, Governor Legarra and four other officials went to the Sonoran capital at Arizpe. Father Gutiérrez had arranged with an attorney to help them prepare a formal petition to be presented to the Intendant Governor of Sonora. It was the friar's intention to ask that the residents of Tumacácori and environs be awarded legal title to mission lands and any additional acreage the Jesuits may have acquired for livestock grazing. The petition was granted on December 17, 1806, and the presidial commander at Tubac, Manuel de León, was instructed to survey and confirm the boundaries of the Tumacácori grant. The survey crew marked out a standard allocation which was chosen to run south along the fertile river all the way to Calabazas. It was less than a half-mile wide, but more than ten miles long. An additional grant of grazing land was surveyed south to Guevavi, bringing the total area to about 6,770 acres. But even as Father Gutiérrez was making certain the rights of Tumacácori's residents would be protected, the mother country of Spain was being invaded. The year was 1809, and once again, events in Europe would have repercussions in tiny Tumacácori.

CHAPTER THIRTEEN

Insurgency

BOURBON SPAIN, WEAK
CONFUSED, AND DIVIDED, FELL TO THE
MIGHT OF NAPOLEON. WITH THE KING OF SPAIN HELD BY THE

French, the rise of guerrilla resistance in the Iberian peninsula, and an attempt by Spain to form a government in exile, there was confusion in New Spain as well. Loyalty to Spain was strong in the north, but farther south there was talk of seizing the moment to strike for independence. Spaniards born in New Spain, the *criollos*, had long suffered under the condescending dominance of the *peninsulares* born in old Spain. The latter traditionally held the reins of power. Moreover, the better educated priests and intellectuals had access to ideas springing from the Enlightenment. These ideas called for governmental, social, and scientific reform, and recent successful revolutions in France and the United States became models for others to emulate.

Just as the new church was being dedicated in Caborca in 1809, a patriotic appeal went out for support of King Ferdinand VII and the resistance government fighting in Spain. All were supposed to contribute, and Father Gutiérrez's hopes for completion of his new church were frustrated once more. Then, on September 16, 1810, hatred in parts of New Spain erupted into violence.

The Mexican Insurgency began as a campaign against the last vestiges of government rooted in the Middle Ages, but it quickly degenerated into a nightmarish race war. A secular priest, Miguel Hidalgo y Costilla, carrying the banner of the Virgin of Guadalupe, led the criollos, Indians, and mestizos. But he could not control them as their smoldering hatred for the peninsulares exploded into a frenzy of bloody butchery. Six months later Father Hidalgo was a prisoner of the royalists, and he was executed in Chihuahua City on July 30, 1811. Although he failed as a military commander, Hidalgo's laudable proposals for social change and for Indians' rights have made him justly revered as the father of Mexican Independence. Others carried on the fight and by the time independence finally came in 1821, much of the passion, and blood, had gone out of the war.

The years of insurrection were hard on the people of the Pimería Alta. In fact, conditions seemed to deteriorate after 1810. Wars on the continent added to the drain on New Spain's resources. The traditional annual mission subsidy of $350 pesos ceased to arrive at Tumacácori after about 1814. Taxes were levied to support a variety of causes, and presidial soldiers were sent southward to fight the insurgents. The only pressure that had eased was that of the Apache. Reduced raiding had permitted the 1808 reoccupation of Calabazas by some of the

increasing numbers of Spaniards moving into the area, who used it as a *rancho*. A gold mine near Guevavi reopened in 1814, employing Yaqui Indian laborers and their families.

During his quarter of a century at Tumacácori, Narciso Gutiérrez had married 97 couples, baptized 255 children, and had buried an equal number, 255, of whom just less than half were younger than sixteen years of age. Father Narciso died December 13, 1820, and was buried in the same tired old Jesuit church alongside his predecessor, his dream of a new church unfulfilled. He had seen many changes since 1794, but at least he was spared the trauma of an independent Mexico, severed from the land of his birth.

CHAPTER FOURTEEN

Mexico Is Born

Toward the end of Mexico's struggle for independence, members of the privileged classes became united, whether clergy, criollos, or peninsulares. To the fore came Agustín de Iturbide with his February 1821 *Plan de Iguala* and its three initial, and principal, provisions: a guarantee of Mexico's immediate and total independence as a constitutional monarchy; the defense of Catholicism as the one true religion; and racial equality. While there were twenty-four articles in the plan, the first three were the most appealing. The green-white-red tricolor representing the three guarantees quickly became the national flag. So universally popular in Mexico were these ideas that Spain had no choice other than to acquiesce. On August 24, 1821, General Juan O'Donojú, who had been sent to Mexico as viceroy but who never assumed the office, signed a treaty with Iturbide which recognized Mexico's independence. It further stipulated that if no European prince could be found to become the king of Mexico, someone else could be appointed.

Rejected by Ferdinand and refused recognition by Spain, the new nation searched for leadership. Iturbide demurely succumbed to prearranged demands that he accept the title of Agustín I, Emperor of Mexico. Concerned more with establishing a royal court than with repairing an economy shattered by ten years of civil war, the new emperor was gone in ten months. In his wake was a legacy of military coup and disregard for law. It would not be too many years before the extreme liberals, who favored a federalist government as opposed to a centralist government, would rule Mexico.

*A*n espada ancha, *typical of early nineteenth century weapons made on the frontier*

CHAPTER FIFTEEN

Father Estelric Works on the Church

WINTER TRAVEL ON
THE NORTH MEXICAN FRONTIER IN THE
EARLY PART OF THE NINETEENTH CENTURY MUST HAVE BEEN

anything but pleasant. It makes one appreciate all the more the 1820-21 visit to the frontier by the Bishop of Sonora, a Carmelite priest named Bernardo del Espíritu Santo, when one considers the cold, the dust, the thirst, and the aching muscles resulting from a bumpy journey that eventually totaled three thousand miles. What is equally remarkable is that the bishop made 60,000 confirmations on this visitation alone. Sixty thousand!

And at Tumacácori, on the first day of January 1821, there to greet his prelate was Tumacácori's new missionary, Juan Bautista Estelric. Father Estelric was a man who was able to accomplish things. Arriving at the mission in December 1820, he realized that Tumacácori's wealth lay in its herds: 5,500 head of cattle; 1,080 sheep; 590 horses; 60 mules; and 20 donkeys. Four hundred and thirteen bushels of wheat in storage would not feed 196 residents until the next harvest. If the people were to eat

and build a church, something had to be done.

The solution to the problem arrived in the person of Don Ignacio Pérez, a prominent Sonoran career officer who wished to become a prominent rancher as well. With some judicious prodding by the Bishop, a contract was signed the day after his arrival, January 2, 1821. In fact, it may well have been the Bishop rather than Father Juan who decided to trade cattle for construction. Don Ignacio bought 4,000 head at three pesos each, one third down and the balance due in two payments within a year and a half. Construction seemed thus assured.

The first payment of $4,000 pesos was made on delivery of the cattle in mid-February and Father Estelric hired Félix Antonio Bustamente from Sombrerete, Zacatecas, as maestro. Father Gutiérrez had managed to raise the new mission's walls to about seven feet, as high as he could go without a maestro. The next courses, at a greater height, would include arches and require scaffolding. Bustamente reviewed the plans and the work that had been completed to that point. He made some suggestions. Given the uncertainty of the times and the money available, why not eliminate the transepts? This would make available those adobes that could be salvaged and would cut back on the numbers of regular adobes and burned bricks needed for walls and vaulting. Estelric agreed. The rest of the plan remained unchanged as maestro Bustamente hired his crew and began.

During the next 6½ months the transepts were closed off, the walls were raised to the fourteen-foot level, and the vault over the sanctuary and the dome of the baptistry were built. This required some 7,000 adobes and 3,100 burned adobes (fired bricks) for the sacristy vault. It also called for lime; sand; scaffolding; buckets; tubs; hides; barrels; handbarrows; picks; shovels; framing for the doors, windows, and vaults; and wages to cover about 160 work days for the crew.

Father Juan overspent his budget by a thousand pesos, counting on that second payment to bail him out. The 16th of August arrived, but the $2,000 pesos did not. Don Ignacio was stalling. With all the turmoil in Mexico, who could tell what might happen to the missions and their debts? Desperate, Estelric wrote a draft for a thousand pesos on Don Ignacio to maestro Bustamente and fired off a strong letter to the recalcitrant rancher. Pérez honored the draft and Bustamente got the money due him, but once again the project ground to a halt when the balance due Tumacácori remained unpaid.

Estelric gave up the fight. By May of 1822, scandal had forced his removal. A woman was involved and there were rumors of two children. Although chastised and turned down in his efforts to be given the chaplaincy at the presidio of Santa Cruz, he managed to keep both ministry and mistress before dying at Guásavas in December of 1835. He was fifty-one years old.

CHAPTER SIXTEEN

Mission Completed

FOR SIXTEEN MONTHS
AFTER HIS ARRIVAL AT TUMACÁCORI
IN MAY 1822, FATHER RAMÓN LIBERÓS DOGGEDLY PURSUED

the wily and elusive Don Ignacio Pérez, as determined to collect the debt as Pérez was to defer it. When Don Ignacio wrote in September promising a thousand pesos in cash and another thousand worth of goods, Liberós believed him and proceeded to act accordingly to complete the church.

In 1822, a significant event occurred that has led to some confusion. On December 13, exactly two years after his death, the remains of Narciso Gutiérrez as well as those of his predecessor Baltasar Carrillo, were dug up from the Jesuit-built mission and reinterred in the new church. It has been suggested that this event coincided with the dedication of the church and that the building was nearly complete. But such was not the case. The barrel vault of the sanctuary and the dome of the baptistry were finished, but the walls were only at the fourteen-foot level.

At some point during his tenure, Father Liberós changed the patronage of Tumacácori, for the third and last time, to that of La Purísima Concepción. It would be tidy had he done so on the Sunday before the reinterment, December 8, the feast day of La Purísima. But Liberós continued to refer to the church as San José

during December, and it is probable that the dedication to La Purísima occurred around 1825-1826. By then the decorations in the sanctuary and the placement of the statuary would have been decided upon, and the rededication probably took place before Father Liberós left in 1828.

As for Father Gutiérrez, it seems somehow appropriate that he was destined to be buried in three separate locations. Only fifty-five when he died in 1820, he was first buried in the Jesuit-built church where he had worked for twenty-six years, San José de Tumacácori. Two years later he was reburied in the floor of the church he had started, La Purísima Concepción de Tumacácori. And finally, in February 1935, he was removed once more and laid to rest — along with Father Carrillo — beneath the floor of the mortuary chapel of the church he had hoped to copy, Mission San Xavier del Bac.

At long last, it appeared as though Tumacácori was going to get its new church. The persistence of Father Liberós paid off, and in September of 1823, Don Rafael Elías González guaranteed payment of the balance due on the sale of the livestock, $6,366 pesos. The tough friar had won. And by now various cost cutting alterations

Sketch by H.M.T. Powell, October 1849

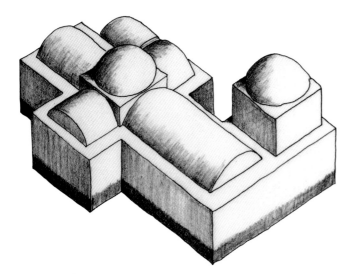

*G*utierrez's original plans for the church in 1801 called for vaulted transepts. Construction according to this plan only reached a height of seven feet.

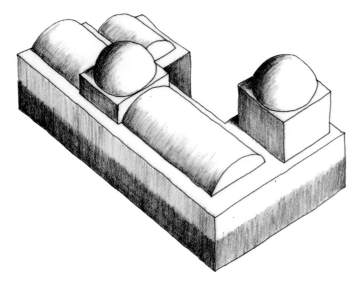

*S*hortness of funds for materials and to hire maestros for the complicated vaulting caused Estelic to accept a simplification of the original plan — the elimination of the vaulted transepts. During this period of construction, the walls reached a height of fourteen feet.

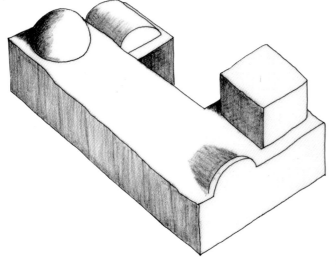

*W*hen construction resumed in September 1823, Liberós proposed several changes that saved money — thinner walls, a dome over the sanctuary, a flat, viga supported roof instead of a vaulted plan. This simplified plan is the church seen today.

in the final plan had been made, producing the church that stands today: thinner walls above fourteen feet, a flat roof, no transepts, and modifications in the choir loft and bell tower. The facade was built, walls rose quickly, thousands of adobes were made and thousands were fired, and huge quantities of lime were produced. Some years ago a park ranger at Tumacácori with time and curiosity estimated that the church contained 1,623 cubic yards of material. This figure does not include any of the other buildings, which would more than double the total.

The dome and roof were probably in place around the end of 1825 when plastering was begun, first on the interior and then on the exterior. The exterior walls were decorated with handfuls of crushed brick pressed into the wet plaster, and the facade was given a distinct and colorful treatment.

During the final three-year building phase, 1825-1828, construction proceeded slowly. Work continued on the third and, as planned, final level of the bell tower. A cylindrical mortuary chapel was built with its entrance facing the gate through the cemetery wall on the west. The entrance was rectangular and projected several feet from the circular body of the chapel. The dome intended for the chapel was never built. The *convento* was probably being overhauled during this period as well.

The area looked good with its gleaming new church, grayish white against a blue sky. Inside, the arch of the choir loft set off the high-ceilinged nave as one entered. The dark red plaster of the floor contrasted nicely with the black dado on the lower portion of the white walls, plain except for the oval stations of the cross, the columned and painted statue niches, and the band of pendant half circles near the ceiling. Additional altars, two on each side, projected into the nave.

Most of the statues in the church were carved in guild workshops in Mexico prior to 1785 and are excellent examples of Mexican baroque religious imagery. How did they come to be at Tumacácori? Styles change, and if a wealthy patron wishes to present a church with a nice new statue, what do you do with the old one? One solution is to send it to the needy missions on the frontier.

When the 1750s Jesuit church of San José de Tumacácori was torn down in the 1820s, it is possible some of its furnishings went elsewhere. Behind the main altar at the former mission church of San Pedro y San Pablo de Tubutama in Sonora's Altar Valley is an eighteenth century *retablo*, or altarpiece, of just the right size for that of the Tumacácori's Jesuit church. It holds five oil paintings depicting scenes in the life of San José. It is entirely possible that this retablo came from Tumacácori.

The sanctuary of Tumacácori's new structure was the most ornately decorated. There were statues, floral stencil work, pictures of the apostles, painted draperies, and geometric designs and bells painted in a variety of reds, blues, greens, and yellows. On each of the four pendentives at the upper corners of the room was a painting representing one of the attributes of the Virgin Mary.

The sacristy was fairly plain, with a few pieces of furniture to hold the various vestments and vessels. From here the priest could enter the pulpit up a short flight of steps. What is now a doorway through the north wall was then a window. From here also a short corridor led to the adjoining convento area on the east side.

The convento was the center of activity for the mission community. Roughly square, an arched arcade with a brick floor laid in a herringbone pattern extended along the west side and part of the north and south wings. On the south side were the priests' living quarters, rooms for visitors, a small chapel, a school room, and a reception area. Across the courtyard to the north were various work rooms and work areas: a grist mill, leather workers' shop, blacksmith, granary, food warehouse, pottery kilns, slaughterhouse, carpenter shop, and a corral for animals. Any or all of these, and more, were possible. It was here, too, on the north side adjoining the two-story warehouse, that the *monjerío* was located, the place where young women learned various crafts. The monjerío was one of two locations in the convento, the other being the priests' quarters, with an indoor toilet. The sewer system was fed from water tanks in front of the present church and emptied into the orchard area.

There were about 5-1/4 acres in the walled orchard and garden area east of the convento. Pomegranates, quinces, and figs were grown and there were over fifty peach trees. Peach pits show up now and then in the adobes of the church walls, and Forty Niners lucky enough to have been passing through during peach season commented on all the delicious fruit with no one but passersby to eat it.

Living quarters for the mission residents formed an almost complete hollow square to the south of the church and convento, done in the same flat-roofed, plastered-adobe style of the convento except for some of those on the south side, which were brush shelters or ramadas. Water for the entire complex was supplied by the nearby Santa Cruz River, a stream which Father Kino had named the Río Santa María. The river in the Santa Cruz Valley flows north, and at Tumacácori it makes a curve to the east. This was bisected by an *acequia*, or irrigation ditch, about two miles long that brought water through the orchard area. Another, smaller, branch of this acequia carried water to the area of the living quarters and to tanks in front of the church. The water table is only about twenty feet below the surface here and hand dug wells are feasible, although none has yet been found.

Completing the mission complex were the communal fields to the south, fenced and well cared for, where wheat and other crops were grown.

Tumacácori finally had a church of which the whole community could be proud.

CHAPTER SEVENTEEN

The Mission Loses Its Priest

LAND OWNERSHIP
PATTERNS EVOLVED WITH THE TIMES
AS MORE AND MORE NON-PIMANS MOVED INTO MISSION

communities, established farms and ranches, or tried their hand at placer mining. Indians in growing numbers were drawn to the wage economy of towns and ranches. In keeping with a growing demand for private ownership, numerous land grants were awarded.

The San Ignacio de la Canoa grant extended north from Tubac's boundary and bordered partly on the lands of Mission San Xavier. Father Juan Vaño of San Xavier tried twice to outbid brothers Tomás and Ignacio Ortiz for the land, but lost. The brothers were awarded the grant in December 1821. Other grants followed: the San José de Sonoita, the San Rafael de la Zanja, the San Bernardino of Ignacio Pérez and the infamous Tumacácori cattle sale, the Buenavista near Guevavi, the San Juan de las Boquillas y Nogales, the San Rafael de Valle, the San Ignacio del Babocómari, and the Tres Alamos.

Father Gutiérrez had helped reestablish Tumacácori's claim to its mission and grazing lands. Father Liberós had helped defend the grant when cattle belonging to Don León Herreros of Tubac grazed some of the land in 1823. The matter was settled amicably, but times were rapidly changing.

The mission community of San Ignacio, some 70 miles south of Tumacácori, was an example of future prospects for Pimans. In 1820 San Ignacio's missionaries were ministering to a total of 1,518 people of whom a mere forty-seven were Indians. Only San Xavier, Tumacácori, and Caborca could claim a majority of Indians in residence at the time.

The great Yaqui Indian revolt of 1825 drew the region's troops to the south. Even so, Liberós seemed unconcerned. "My Pimas," he wrote in a letter to a friend, "have not a care in the world. They are dancing vigorously and

practicing for the *matachines*. Already they do it well...." They were Yaqui miners and laborers who brought the elaborate *matachín* dance ritual, a devotion to the Virgin, to what is now Arizona. This devotional dance continues among Arizona's Yaquis, another unbroken link in the region's long chain of cultural continuity.

Spain steadfastly refused to recognize an independent Mexico, and there were rumors that Ferdinand VII might try to reclaim it. None of this contributed to the popularity of the peninsulares, and finally the long-expected law was passed: Spaniard, go home. Patriotic fervor swept northward, and once again the distasteful job of expelling the foreign-born missionaries fell upon the presidial commander. This time it was Captain Pedro Villaescusa of Tucson who told Ramón Liberós he had three days in which to get the affairs of Tumacácori in order and to get out. Liberós was not about to leave the mission complex and its lands in the hands of non-Indians. He named Ramón Pamplona administrator of the mission. Pamplona, half Papago and half Yaqui, was born at the mission in 1785 and had been its governor since Liberós's arrival. He had been one of the representatives with the land grant delegation in 1806 and his son Ignacio would serve as governor of Tumacácori in the 1840s.

Thus it was that during the second week of April, 1828, the last resident friar left Tumacácori. Scaffolding still covered the nearly finished bell tower and the mortuary chapel, but the church and convento were in excellent shape. The statue niches in the bell tower had just received their plaster shell designs symbolic of the patron saint of Spain, Santiago de Compostela. Tumacácori had nearly reached the peak that had been dreamed for it; now it would begin a downhill slide to abandonment and decay.

Just before leaving, Father Ramón finished his records with this note on a clean sheet of paper: "Having concluded these books [mission registers] and got out another to follow, leaving the latter one just in case, and having burned the papers of my personal administration, I am about to set out on my journey."

CHAPTER EIGHTEEN

The Final Mission Years

Four priests were now left in the Pimería Alta. They were José Pérez Llera at San Ignacio, Faustino Gonzáles at Caborca, Juan Maldonado for Oquitoa and Tubutama, and, at Cocóspera, Rafael Díaz. Díaz was also charged with looking after Tumacácori, San Xavier, and the presidios of Santa Cruz, Tubac, and Tucson.

Civil administrators arrived to pick the bones of the relatively helpless missions, assembling lists of debts and exacting payment from dwindling mission supplies. By the time the mission properties were returned to the care of the friars in 1830, Tumacácori had 400 head of cattle running wild. There were a few remaining horses and some 800 sheep, and most of the wheat fields were uncultivated. Ramón Pamplona had done what he could and was justly praised for his accomplishments. He had been relatively powerless, however, to prevent abuses by the interim administrator appointed after he had resigned.

More serious than the threat of civilian abuse of the mission was the increasing threat of Apache raiding. Sáric, for example, a mission settlement on the Río Altar, had been abandoned in 1828, the same year that a Sonoran state militia was established. Apache dependence on the presidios for gifts had begun to erode following Mexican independence, and by 1830 raiding had once again become a full time occupation for them. It began to look like a race to see who could finish off the remaining mission property, the civilian settlers or the raiders. Tumacácori would surely have perished had it not been for the fact that five hundred people still lived in and around the presidio of Tubac. Better to have settlers than raiders as constant companions.

As if this weren't enough, by 1833 the political situation in Sonora had become horrendous, with arguments over where to locate the state's capital reaching blood-

The facade of Tubutama, Sonora, photographed by George Grant in 1935

33

letting stages. Added to this were yet another Yaqui uprising and a national revolt that put López de Santa Anna and a new government in power in Mexico City. The professional soldiers on the frontier, constantly short of everything, especially pay, staged a successful revolt against the commanding officer of Sonora.

It was becoming difficult to find anyone in the region who was happy and content, or so it seemed. The seeds of the next Piman rebellion were sprouting, and in 1835 the governors of the Papago communities of Caborca and Pitiquito and the captain general of the Pimas and Papagos set forth grievances in a letter. The Indians had been driven from San Ignacio and were almost gone from Sáric, Tubutama, and Oquitoa. The peaceful Apaches living near Tucson were encroaching on Papago lands. Murders and retaliatory raids had occurred near Altar. The Papagos feared they might be forced to adopt the tactics of the Apaches in order to survive.

The change of national government from federalist to centralist, as embodied in Santa Anna's ascent to power, propelled Texans on a path to independence from Mexico. To the west, the whole Sonoran world seemed in turmoil, with 1837 bringing the beginnings of a destructive feud between two groups that would last a generation and sap the strength of political factions led by Manuel Gándara and José Urrea. Pressures on Indians from miners and settlers in the western Pimería continued until finally the third Piman revolt erupted in May of 1840.

After years of increased pressures on their land and water, Indian frustration boiled over at the settlement of Cóbota, a community northwest of Sáric. More than a hundred rebellious Papagos fought a battle with Mexicans and other Papagos, and from then until June 1843, there were major campaigns until everyone finally had enough and the third Piman revolt came to an end.

The 1840s saw a slow, sporadic, but persistent migration of middle Santa Cruz Valley residents to Tucson to escape raiding and to find work. The militia did what it could, but it was never enough. Many Apaches were peacefully settled in towns — 169 of them living in Tubac in 1843, for example — and some of their number were willing allies of the Mexicans and Pimans. But hostile Apaches seemed to be everywhere.

Fairly typical of campaigns against the Apaches was one that began November 29, 1845, and which ended on December 7. Of the 155 men involved, 60 were soldiers from Tucson, 23 soldiers came from Tubac, 20 civilians who lived in Tucson, and 35 Apaches and 17 Pimas from San Xavier. They swept north to the Gila River, east to the San Pedro River, down to the mouth of Arivaipa Creek, and home. Their efforts produced nine hostile Apache casualties.

If one word could summarize this period it would probably be "deterioration." The once proud Mission La Purísima Concepción de Tumacácori was no exception. A report filed by the Tubac justice of the peace in April 1843 painted a sad picture: the buildings in the convento were "for the most part fallen down and threatened with ruin," although the church was in good condition. The fields a mile-and-a-half south and on the east side of the river were filled with mesquite, and because of the shortage of water, the remaining Indians cultivated only their own fields.

The Franciscans were giving up, too. Antonio Gonzáles, the last resident Franciscan in the Pimería Alta, left San Ignacio in 1843. This ended seventy-five years of missionary work by the gray robes in the Pimería Alta. The missions were secularized by default, and would be served by the parish priest from San Ignacio, Bachiller Don Trinidad García Rojas.

The people living at Tumacácori would have been surprised to learn, if anyone had bothered to tell them, that the land on which they and their ancestors had been living for the past untold centuries was now officially abandoned. And adding insult to injury, it was valued at less than $500 pesos. An early Arizona land speculation project was about to unfold, this time with no priest to interfere and with title documents conveniently missing.

Only one bidder for the Tumacácori lands showed up at the Sonoran city of Guaymas where the sale was to occur. Based on the law of 1837 and a decree of 1842, unclaimed mission lands whose value did not exceed $500 pesos could be sold at public auction. The lone bidder was Francisco Alejandro Aguilar. Coincidentally, he was also the brother-in-law of, and agent for, Manuel María Gándara y Gortari, off-and-on Governor of Sonora, rebel, military commander, stockman, and all around wily politician. Even though Gándara acquired the property, there was no rush to evict its residents. Perhaps the Apaches would do it for him. They certainly slowed Gándara's occupation of the land, and it wasn't until 1853 that he was able to establish a ranching operation at Calabazas, a part of the Tumacácori estate.

CHAPTER NINETEEN

An Era Ends

By THE MID-NINE-

TEENTH CENTURY, MEXICO WAS IN

DESPERATE NEED OF SO MANY THINGS, BUT A WAR WAS NOT

one of them. With the annexation of Texas in 1845 by the expansive United States and the resulting boundary problems between the United States and Mexico, it was inevitable there would be trouble. It came when Americans began to build a fort on lands Mexico felt were rightly hers and when eleven soldiers of an American scouting party were killed in an ambush by Mexican troops. The United States declared war on Mexico in May of 1846. Mexico returned the favor on July 2, a brash action considering there were only $1,839 pesos in the national treasury and there was little in place that could properly be called a government.

As the well-equipped American armies marched down from the north, Santa Anna allowed himself to be persuaded to accept his country's presidency once more. Whatever else Santa Anna may have been, he was a good organizer. With no money, he was able to put together an army of 18,000 men. He drove them north, freezing and starving, losing 4,000 to desertion, disease, and hunger. He faced General Zachary Taylor at Buena Vista on February 22, 1846. Desperate and decimated by U.S. artillery, they lost another 1,500 men as they fought until they dropped. Taylor was stopped for the moment, but the Mexicans had to withdraw. The battle of Buena Vista had been won by valor but lost by reality. Within two years, Mexico was defeated, a victim of poverty,

apathy, despair, and internal jealousies and hatred. The Treaty of Guadalupe Hidalgo, signed in 1848, cost Mexico half of her lands.

During the United States and Mexican War, the Mormon Battalion under Lieutenant Colonel Philip St. George Cooke marched into Tucson, Sonora, in December 1846, headed for California. No one seemed anxious for a fight. The Mexican troops protecting Tucson withdrew a bit to the south and Cooke seemed in no rush to find them. He preferred to enjoy Tucson's hospitality and to move on after twenty-four hours.

Father García Rojas visited Tumacácori on February 14, 1847, and baptized six people. Three months later, Manuel Gándara, the owner of the "abandoned" mission property, took office as the duly elected governor of Sonora, a position that he or a surrogate would hold for most of the next decade.

The Sonoran frontier was badly hurt when the U.S. Navy blockaded the port of Guaymas between October 1847 and June 1848. This cut the flow of supplies to the north, and with no duties being collected, troops were not being fed, much less paid. Apache pressures increased, further impoverishing the region. And to add to the turmoil and uncertainty a rush for California's gold began in October 1848. Within five months, some 5,000 Mexicans headed northwest, severely draining needed manpower from Sonora.

It was also in October of 1848 that the soldiers with Major L.P. Graham, returning from fighting in the south, traveled down the Santa Cruz Valley enroute to California. Major Graham has been immortalized in print for his remarkable ability to stay drunk, while his more sober and literate junior officer, Lieutenant Cave Johnson Couts, was the officer who did the immortalizing. Couts kept a careful written record of the journey, one published in this century. The troops passed many deserted ranches, found the beleaguered presidio at Santa Cruz suffering from persistent Apache attacks, encountered some twenty miners near Guevavi (who would soon be driven out by Apaches), and, on October 22, passed through Tumacácori:

"The churches in this valley are remarkable," wrote Couts. "At Tumacácori is a very large and fine church standing in the midst of a few common conical Indian huts, made of bushes, thatched with grass, huts of the most common and primitive kind...This Church is now taken care of by the Indians, Pimas, most of whom are off attending a jubilee, or fair, on the other side of the mountain.

"No priest has been in attendance for many years, though all its images, pictures, figures &c remain unmolested, and in good keeping. No Mexicans live with them at all."

The "jubilee, or fair" was quite possibly being held in Magdalena, as it still is each year in October.

The desolation observed by Couts was widespread. An 1848 census of Sonora stated that Apache raids had caused the depopulation of twenty-six mining camps, thirty haciendas, and ninety ranches. There were still 249 people in Tubac, mostly Apaches, and Tucson had only 760. There were probably no more than two dozen people left at Tumacácori.

CHAPTER TWENTY

Abandonment

At Eight o'Clock

ON THE EVENING OF SATURDAY, DEC-
EMBER 9, 1848 A MESSENGER ARRIVED AT THE QUARTERS

of Captain Antonio Comadurán, commander of the Tucson presidio. Tubac was being decimated by Apaches and several soldiers and civilians were already dead. By the time Captain Comadurán could assemble a few volunteers, the attack was over. All that could be done was to survey the destruction.

That was it. Enough. No more. The survivors at Tubac packed their belonging and headed through the bitter cold to Tucson. The few people left at Tumacácori moved to San Xavier. The *santos* (statues and images of saints), vestments, and sacred vessels were carefully packed to be deposited temporarily at Mission San Xavier for safekeeping. In 1855, Ensign Joaquín Comadurán, Antonio's son, meticulously inventoried the church furnishings from Tumacácori that were at San Xavier.

The hoped for springtime return to Tumacácori never came, although in ensuing years former residents made several attempts to reestablish their claim to the mission and its lands.

For the next six decades the winds of change would whisper through the adobe walls as history unfolded. Forty Niners headed past the ruins as they traveled down the Santa Cruz enroute to California. The Gadsden Purchase added southern Arizona, and Tumacácori, to the United States in June of 1854. An Anglo company put its mining headquarters at Tubac. The Civil War in the United States saw troops from both South and North in the territory. More settlers moved in. Through it all, Apaches, Apaches, Apaches, until finally, in 1886, the band of Chiricahua Apaches led by Geronimo and Naiche surrendered for the last time. The Apache wars came to an end. But Tumacácori remained abandoned and forlorn.

37

CHAPTER TWENTY-ONE
Tumacácori Becomes a National Monument

"Calabasas, Arizona

"June 30, 1908

"Subject to the acceptance thereof by the Secretary of the Interior, under the terms of the provisions of the Act of Congress approved June 8, 1906 (34 Stat., 235), entitled 'An Act for the Protection of American Antiquities,' and for the purposes specified in said act, I hereby relinquish to the United States the E 1/2 of the NW 1/4 of the SW 1/4 of the SE 1/4, and the W 1/2 of the NE 1/4 of the SW 1/4 of the SE 1/4 of Section 30, in Township 21 South, Range 13 East, Gila and Salt River Meridian, Arizona, containing 10 acres, the same being embraced within my homestead entry No. 3035.

"his
"Carmen X Mendez
"mark

"Witnesses:
"C.H. Willimas
"Frank J. Duffy"

There was no way that Carmen Méndez could have known when he filed his homestead application for 160 acres in 1899, nor nine years later when he relinquished ten of them to the government, that his claim would be invalidated by the heirs of Luis María Baca because of a land grant in New Mexico. This caused Tumacacori National Monument to be established twice, first by Executive Order of President Theodore Roosevelt on September 15, 1908, and again on December 8, 1917, when the owners who had acquired these Baca lands transferred the monument back to the United States with a quit-claim deed.

At the time of President Roosevelt's Executive Order, there was no National Park Service. So Tumacácori was cared for by the nearest federal agency, the Forest Service, a branch of the Department of Agriculture. Carmen Méndez, the Arizona Pioneers' Historical Society, the Forest Service, and several local groups and individuals were interested in the preservation of the ruins. It was the original donation of the ten-acre site by the Méndez family that made this possible.

The story of how the heirs of New Mexico's Baca family subsequently came into possession of the land is a fascinating one. On January 16, 1821, the legislature of Durango granted a tract of land in northeastern New Mexico to Luis María Baca. Fourteen years later, the Mexican government awarded part of the grant to colonists who founded what became the town of Las Vegas. After the Treaty of Guadalupe Hidalgo was ratified, the Baca heirs presented their claim to the United States Congress, which allowed them to select in five detached parts a quantity of New Mexico land elsewhere in the public domain equal to that which they had lost. Before 1863, Arizona was part of the Territory of New Mexico. These detached segments were called "floats." The 100,000-acre segment they selected in southern Arizona encompassed much of the Tumacácori-Tubac-Calabazas area. It became known as Baca Float No. 3.

A survey of Baca Float No. 3 was ordered in 1864. Apaches killed William Wrightson and other members of his survey party and the survey was not completed. Subsequently, there were sales of land, disputes concerning locations of survey markers, denials of various claims because of legal technicalities, approval of claims, overturned decisions, and so on. The Secretary of the Interior finally announced he would dispose of the land via homestead laws, and it was then that Carmen Méndez filed his claim. The Baca case continued through the courts, however and on June 22, 1914, the Supreme Court dealt a shocking blow to the sixty or more people who were happily going about their business in the belief they were secure in the title to their lands. The 94,289 acres of Baca Float No. 3 were awarded to claimants James E. Bouldin, Jennie N. Bouldin, Helen Lee Bouldin,

and Eldon M. Bailey. The government had lost title to Tumacacori National Monument.

The displaced landowners were allowed to select land elsewhere, and no one seemed too concerned about the status of the national monument. But everything fell into place when the Bouldins' and Baileys' quit-claim deed to Tumacácori was recorded in 1917. The Solicitor General said there was no need to proclaim Tumacacori National Monument a second time, and with this final decision in April of 1918 the years of confusion over land titles came to an end.

CHAPTER TWENTY-TWO

The Era of "Boss" Pinkley

BORN ON A FARM IN
MISSOURI, FRANK PINKLEY WENT
TO PHOENIX AT AGE NINETEEN TO SEEK A CURE FOR HIS

tuberculosis and to try his hand at farming. In 1901, just a year after his arrival, he was offered the job as caretaker and watchman at Casa Grande National Monument. A tent was provided for housing but he had to dig his own well. Neighbors were few and far between, but one of them, a schoolteacher, had a daughter. In 1906 Frank Pinkley and Edna Townsend were married.

With its creation in 1916 the new National Park Service found itself in charge of several national monuments scattered throughout the Southwest. One of these was Tumacacori, and in December 1918, Pinkley was named its custodian in addition to his duties at Casa Grande. He immediately began cleanup and stabilization after his initial inspection trip.

Pinkley's work at Tumacacori was impressive. In these early days of the National Park Service there was usually just one man stationed at each of the smaller monuments, and heaven help him if he weren't married. It was the wife, the HCWP (Honorary Custodian Without Pay), who helped fix leaky roofs and water lines, assisted with tours and paperwork, and who ran the area when her husband went to town for supplies. Pinkley had to solicit support from various civic groups to complete his major stabilization project at Tumacácori. He hired laborers, wrote reports, pored over volumes of published works

that hinted at Tumacácori's history, talked with everyone who might know anything about the place, supervised directly when he could the massive chore of cleanup and stabilization of the ravaged ruin, and somehow still found time to take a trip in 1921 with Edna and their two children — at his own expense and wearing a Park Service uniform — to California to compare Tumacácori with California missions. And all of this was in addition to his work at Casa Grande Monument.

Major work on Tumacácori's church took place in 1920-1921. The National Park Service could furnish only $1,095 for the project. An additional $1,060 came from the Phoenix and Tucson Knights of Columbus, the Arizona Archaeological and Historical Society, and the Nogales Chamber of Commerce. The latter even met the payrolls for a time. The walls of the church were restored to their original height, the arched pediment of the facade was replaced, support for the bell tower was restored, and a roof was installed. The original roof was gone by the mid-1850s. The roof installed by Pinkley was designed by noted Tucson architect, and one-time mayor, Henry O. Jaastad. It was based on original roofing material located by Pinkley and involved almost as much hand labor as had the original roof. Ponderosa pine timbers, copies of the originals, were brought from the

Santa Rita Mountains to the northeast, dressed out by hand, and hoisted into place. Ocotillo stalks gave the ceiling the proper rustic look and hid the modern board, tar, and gravel roof. Pinkley's roof lasted until 1947 when it had to be replaced.

A series of improvements was made in the 1930s for better interpretation of the area's history and for visitor comfort, beginning appropriately enough with rest rooms in 1930. In 1931, 1932, and 1959 residences were built that can be rented by staff members, and in 1935 a wall was constructed to enclose the monument on two sides and part of a third. But one of the biggest projects was that of the visitor center and museum, built in 1937.

For eighteen days starting on October 12, 1935, a National Park Service expedition examined mission churches in northern Sonora despite an insurrection during which the *presidente municipal* (mayor) and chief of police of Santa Ana were murdered. Troops were rushed to Hermosillo, Nogales, Magdalena, Santa Ana, and Altar. All the churches had been closed and their furnishings removed the previous December by the Mexican government.

Undaunted, the intrepid group drove south in two government cars. Their purpose was to collect architectural and historical data that could be used in, among other things, construction of a museum-visitor center-office building at Tumacacori National Monument.

Various plans for the building were proposed, some simple and some rather grandiose. A compromise was finally reached and a set of plans was approved by Frank Pinkley. An allotment of Public Works funds was approved by the Secretary of the Interior in August 1936, and in June of the next year the contract was let to the M.M. Sundt Construction Company of Tucson. Two months later, despite a tremendous rainstorm that ruined the first batch of adobes, construction began. Another contract was simultaneously let with Citizens Utility Company of Nogales, and electricity finally reached the monument. The building was constructed at a cost of $28,992.91. The work was completed and accepted in December 1937.

Many of the architectural features of the museum and visitor center were copied from other mission churches. The shell design over the entrance door is a replica of that at Mission Cocóspera. The front doors, made by the Civilian Conservation Corps (CCC) at Bandelier National Monument in New Mexico, were patterned after those on the church at San Ignacio. Designs for the other doors and for the arcades were borrowed from

Caborca. Oquitoa provided the model for the ceiling in the lobby, and the wooden grill work on the west office window was copied from the choir loft at Tubutama.

Meanwhile, exhibits for the museum were being professionally researched and assembled by the National Park Service at its museum laboratory in Berkeley, California, and during the summer of 1938 installation began. The museum was completed in February 1939, and the next month landscaping of the patio garden was started. The CCC workers who did the work finished in March of the following year.

The most extensive archeological project at Tumacacori was carried out in 1934 and 1935. Using local day labor, Paul Beaubien was charged with locating the walls of subsurface structures associated with the main church building. More than seventy such structures were identified before time and money ran out. Beaubien's report leaves its reader wondering how so much archeology could possibly have been accomplished. When Beaubien arrived in December 1934, the project was well underway, with Walter G. Atwell in charge. Atwell had already exposed the foundations of the 1750s Jesuit church of San José de Tumacácori.

Beaubien supervised shifts of anywhere from two to thirty-five men who were hired for three-day periods with Federal Emergency Relief Act money. He was supposed to locate walls and not excavate rooms completely. He had to backfill as quickly as engineers could do their mapping, and engineers' visits were sporadic. Visitors had a tendency to want to get close to the excavations, which resulted in some damage to the site. Further complications frustrated the archeologist: an extensive network of holes dug by treasure hunters had destroyed history as greed defied logic in futile searches for non-existent mission gold.

In the meantime, Pinkley had become the general superintendent of Southwestern National Monuments, a cluster of Park Service areas that totaled twenty-seven by the year 1940. For many years, Pinkley, who came to be known affectionately among Park Service employees as "the Boss," had worked to get all of his custodians together for a "school of instruction." Approval was finally given, all the details were worked out, and the great day, February 14, 1940, arrived at last. Everyone assembled at headquarters in Coolidge. Pinkley, in uniform, delivered a warm welcoming speech to his men, finished, sat down, and died of a heart attack. If anyone is to be identified as Tumacácori's twentieth-century savior, it would have to be Frank Pinkley.

41

CHAPTER TWENTY-THREE

Preserving Tumacácori

PRESERVATION AND STABILIZATION ARE THE WORDS DE- SCRIBING THE NATIONAL PARK SERVICE'S POLICY WITH REGARD

to Tumacácori. Restoration and reconstruction are not in the plans, nor have they been since the initial cleanup in 1919 and the reroofing of the nave and restoration of the arched pediment on the facade. The goal now, as it has been for decades, is to save what is here.

In the past, this has included the use of Portland cement to protect the adobe from the weather. Over the years the use of cement actually contributed to the decay of the ruins. Moisture became trapped in the walls, and after much testing and many attempts to correct the problem, a team of experts was hired to make recommendations. The answer proved to be simple: tear off everything and go back to using native materials. Or, as Tucson architect Eleazar D. Herreras put it, "Use

what's in the earth around you." And that is precisely what happened.

In 1975 the most comprehensive stabilization program ever attempted at Tumacácori began. A variety of experts from universities and laboratories around the country offered opinions, made tests, and suggested various solutions. The original concept was carried out, however, and the cement was removed from the walls and replaced with mud adobes and lime plaster. When the walls could breath again they dried out. Routine maintenance now replaces new plaster as it spalls off during winter freeze-thaw cycles.

A special part of this project involved work done in the summer of 1982 to reattach loose portions of the

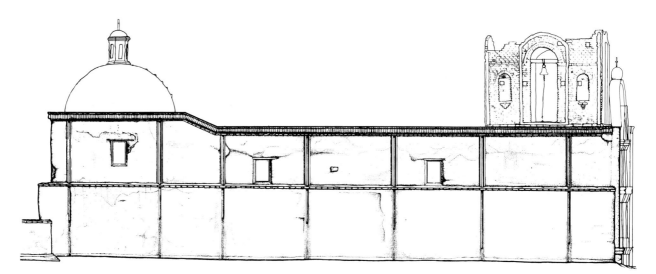

West elevation of church

gypsum wash and paint layers on the dome above the sanctuary. A team of three people from the International Center for the study of the Preservation and Restoration of Cultural Properties (ICCROM) in Rome, Italy, directed and trained seven Park Service conservators.

Some conservation techniques have become simplified over the years. Where strength was formerly the approach, involving the use of nails, concrete, and steel mesh, the modern approach is to make the repairs weaker than the original. If anything goes, it will be the repair.

Five of the statues which had been taken by the Indians from Tumacácori to San Xavier de Bac for safekeeping in 1848 were returned to Tumacácori in 1973, a lapse of 125 years. Two of Tumacácori's principal santos, those of La Purísima Concepción and of San José, remain in daily use at Mission San Xavier. San José is in a niche on the north wall of San Xavier's west transept; La Purísima Concepción is in a corresponding niche in the east transept.

Tumacácori will not be restored. It will be preserved as it is, the physical remains of a nineteenth century frontier mission community. What visitors see today is what their parents may have seen. It is for the visitor that the National Park Service preserves and presents this important part of our nation's cultural heritage. Those who enter the visitor center follow a time line to the past. Those who leave follow the same time line from the present to the future. Here are more than 150 years of birth, life, and death. It is a heritage that belongs to all of us.

*P*reservation work, 1978 and 1979

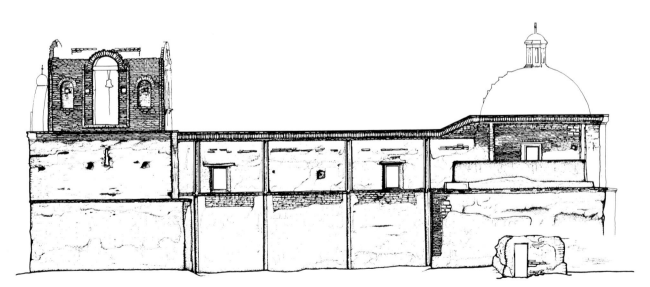

*E*ast elevation of church

43

CHAPTER TWENTY-FOUR

Epilogue

CHANGES IN THE SAN-
TA CRUZ VALLEY IN THE VICINITY OF
OF TUMACÁCORI BECOME OBVIOUS AS MORE AND MORE PEOPLE

move here to work, to build houses, and to retire. Continuity between present and past is subtle, but it exits. There are still cattle and chickens and horses and dogs and crops. There are the soft sounds of spoken Spanish. What is now an interstate highway has always been a major route, even if a slower one. Those who leave the interstate to visit Tubac, Carmen, and Tumacacori will notice adobe buildings and well-kept family yard shrines. And still to be eaten are tortillas, beef, and chiles in recipes which have lasted from the days of Spain's dominance. Pageantry and ritual remain alive at December's annual Fiesta de Tumacácori with its solemn procession to mass. Matachín ceremonies mentioned by Father Liberós in 1825 are still danced at the church on this day. The bishop continues to visit.

The past lives on. Visitors are invited to pause, to savor it.

Reading List

BOLTON, HERBERT E. *Rim of Christendom*, New York, The MacMillan Co., 1936.

FONTANA, BERNARD L. *Of Earth and Little Rain, The Papago Indians*, photographs by John P. Schaefer, Flagstaff: Northland Press, 1981.

GRIFFITH, JAMES S. *Southern Arizona Folk Arts*, Tucson, University of Arizona Press, 1988.

KESSELL, JOHN L. *Mission of Sorrows, Jesuit Guevavi and the Pimas, 1691-1767*, University of Arizona Press, 1970.

KESSELL, JOHN L. *Friars, Soldiers and Reformers, Hispanic Arizona and the Sonora Mission Frontier, 1767-1856*; University of Arizona Press, 1976.

OFFICER, JAMES E. *Hispanic Arizona, 1536-1856*, University of Arizona Press, 1987.

POLZER, CHARLES W. *Kino Guide II*, Southwestern Mission Research Center, 1988.

SPICER, EDWARD H. *Cycles of Conquest, The Impact of Spain, Mexico and the United States on the Indians of the Southwest, 1533-1960*, University of Arizona Press, 1962.

UDALL, STEWART L. *To the Inland Empire, Coronado and Our Spanish Legacy*, photographs by Jerry Jacka; Garden City: Doubleday and Company, 1987.

Acknowledgments

This is one of those "as told to" booklets where someone else does the work. In this case it was Anita Antone, Bill Brown, Tony Crosby, Bunny Fontana, Gloria Giffords, Jim Griffith, Bill Hoy, Jake Ivey, John Kessell, Kieran McCarty, Buzz McHenry, Jim Officer, Charlie Polzer, Cynthia Radding, David Shaul, the late Ned Spicer, Stewart Udall and Jack Williams. Thanks, friends. And thanks to Mary Lou Gortarez, Charlie Hill, Tanner Pilley, T.J. Priehs, Jim Troutwine, Kim Yubeta, and especially to Birdie Stabel, for trying, all of you, to keep me honest.

My friend Manuel Contreras, born in Cucurpe of Opata heritage, veteran of Chennault's Flying Tigers in China, and protector of Tumacácori for twenty years, personifies the contents of this booklet, which is dedicated to him.

Glossary

cabecera, the principal church of a district, with a resident priest.

campo santo, "holy field," cemetery.

convento, the compound adjacent to the mission church, containing the workshops and priests' living quarters.

dado, the decorated lower portion of an interior wall.

Franciscan, a member of the Order of Friars Minor (O.F.M.), a Roman Catholic religious order founded by St. Francis of Assisi in 1209.

Jesuit, a member of the Society of Jesus, a Roman Catholic religious order established by St. Ignatius Loyola.

league, a unit of linear measure equal to about 2.6 miles.

nave, the long central portion of the church.

pendentive, the spherical triangle formed by the junction of a dome to columns or straight walls.

pesos, the monetary unit of Mexico.

Pimería Alta, Upper Pima country, referring to the area in which the northerly of the Pima group lived.

presidio, a military fort.

retablo, an altar screen or altarpiece.

sacristy, a room adjacent to the sanctuary where priests prepare for services.

sanctuary, the most sacred part of the church, containing the main altar.

santo, saint, a religious statue.

viga, an exposed wooden beam.

visita, a village visited by the priest from the cabecera.

Chronology

1492	October, the first 90 Spaniards arrive in the "New" World
1521	Aztec empire destroyed
1540	Society of Jesus established
1540-42	Coronado and his men explore from California to Kansas
1572	Jesuits arrive in New Spain
1598	First Spanish settlement established in New Mexico
1629	Spanish Franciscans at Hopi villages in northern Arizona
1680	Pueblo revolt in New Mexico
1687	Jesuits arrive in Pimería Alta

Spanish era

1691	Kino and Salvatierra visit Tumacácori and Guevavi
1695	First Pima revolt
1701	Guevavi designated a cabecera
1711	March 15, death of Eusebio Francisco Kino
1726	April, Tubac enters recorded history
1736	October, silver discovered at Planchas o Bolas de Plata
1751	November, second Pima revolt
1753	March, presidio being built at Tubac; Tumacácori moves
1756	Calabazas enters recorded history
1767	Expulsion of the Jesuits
1768	Franciscans arrive at former Jesuit missions
1771	Guevavi abandoned, cabecera moved to Tumacácori
1773	Sonoita abandoned
1775-76	De Anza and 240 settlers establish San Francisco
1786	Calabazas abandoned as visita of Tumacácori
1802	Construction begins on new Tumacácori church, suspended later in the year
1807	Tumacácori grant reestablished
1808	Calabazas reoccupied as a rancho
1810	September 16, revolution in Mexico
1821	Second period of construction begins and ends on Tumacácori church
1821	September, Mexican Independence

1899